ISBN 0-88862-048-9

Cover design by Roy Peterson
Design by Lynn Campbell

James Lewis & Samuel, Publishers
35 Britain Street
Toronto

Printed and bound in Canada

FROG FABLES & BEAVER TALES

STANLEY BURKE

ROY PETERSON

James Lewis & Samuel, Publishers
Toronto 1973

Once upon a time long ago there dwelt a race of Beavers.

These industrious animals lived in a faraway Swamp called Canada, where they built dams and cut down trees and were prosperous and happy.

They wished all the other animals in the world could be as happy as they were. So the Beavers would go to the United Assembly of all the animals and say, "Love one another and be like us."

But the other animals were quarrelsome and did not love one another and the Beavers would go away saddened.

On one great occasion a wise Beaver named Lester persuaded the United Assembly to form an animal army to keep the peace. The other animals thought this was such a wonderful idea that they gave Lester the Noble Prize, the highest honor in all the forest.

This pleased the Beavers enormously. They went around slapping their tails and telling one another what wonderful animals they were.

Soon young Beavers were all over the world keeping the peace.

It *was* very noble, but the Beavers were modest—they said it was simply that they were more sensible than other animals.

For a time the United Assembly's animal army was successful, but gradually the other animals tired of the effort. Finally, the peacekeepers were sent home.

This saddened the Beavers and they wondered, "Why can't everyone be like us?"

But they decided to be sensible about it and keep to themselves. After all, in a sad, mad world, they still had the peace and beauty of the Swamp which they shared with the lesser creatures— the Muskrats and the Water Rats and the high-spirited Frogs who made the Swamp ring with their music.

There were also the fun-loving Otters, who lived on the west side of the Swamp, and their friends, the Gophers.

And the Turtles, the original inhabitants, who had been there long before the others arrived.

The Beavers were happy in their Swamp and, protected by the dam, they thought that their happiness would last forever. Alas, it was not to be!

It was all the fault of the Paranoid Eagles and the Perfidious Frogs.

To the south of the Swamp, you see, lived the Eagles, the richest and most powerful of the animals, who ranged on their great wings out across the forest and waste lands beyond, seeking always and everywhere to make a killing.

They were very good at it and they attributed their success to their system and their way of life. Under this system, the biggest and strongest Eagles lived in the tops of the trees and ate the best food, while the other Eagles lived in the lower branches and ate what was left over. The Eagles called this Equality of Opportunity, saying that every Eagle had the same opportunity to be big and strong and to get to the top of the tree. They wanted animals everywhere to have this wonderful system and to be as happy as they were.

Unfortunately, the Eagles had enemies called Bears who had a different idea.

The Bears said that all animals were equal, and that all should have an equal share of the food and should live in the same-sized dens.

The Eagles said that this idea was evil and would destroy freedom. And they said that all the animals must struggle against it.

All young Eagles were trained for combat and every day they flew patrols far to the North over the Land of the Bears to see what they were up to.

The Eagles were fanatical.

They looked for enemies everywhere.

They watched everything.

They listened to everyone.

Their friends. The other Eagles. The white-headed Eagles watched the black-headed Eagles and the black-headed Eagles watched the white-headed Eagles.

No one could be trusted.

Not even the Chief Eagle himself.

All this puzzled and worried the Swamp Creatures. The Eagles told them that the Bears were their enemies too, but the Swamp Creatures were not sure. The Bears, they knew, had never started an animal war, and they had certainly never harmed the creatures of the Swamp. What's more, none of the Swamp Creatures had ever even seen a Bear.

Eagles, however, were all too familiar. They were seen everywhere and they controlled everything, including the poplar trees which the Beavers needed for food.

"We are slaves to the Eagles!" wailed the Beavers. "What shall we do?"

The Beavers held meetings, made speeches, and slapped their tails in anguish but they were no match for the great predators from the South.

And then came the betrayal by the Perfidious Frogs, which was the cruellest blow of all.

The Frogs, you see, were unreasonable.

In ancient times they had been owners of the Swamp. Then the Beavers came and took it and the Frogs never forgave them.

The Beavers said that this was unreasonable because they had been kind to the Frogs. They had even allowed them to help run the Swamp, and had given them important posts like being Chief Minister in Charge of Delivering Messages. "Above all," said the Beavers, "we built the dam which benefits the Frogs so much. They should be grateful."

But the Frogs never forgot and never forgave and the Beavers said that this was silly because it all happened so long ago, and why couldn't the Frogs forget a little thing like being conquered?

The fault, the Beavers said, must lie with the Frog leaders, in particular a nasty little Frog named René.

It wasn't like this before René came along," the Beavers said. "The Frogs used to be happy. They used to sing and dance and they did not bother about dams and things they do not understand. Frogs are not good engineers. They should leave these things to us."

But, while the Beavers were annoyed, they were not worried because, as they said, "What can the Frogs do about it? After all, we control the dam. No dam—no water. No water—no food."

The Frogs, however, became more and more unhappy and, up at the shallow end where they lived, they began to croak:

"Sep-ar-*ate!* Sep-ar-*ate!*"

Booming voices reverberated through the Swamp:

"Sep-ar-*ATE!* SEP-AR-*ATE!*"

Soon it was a never-ending chorus.

"Ridiculous!" gnashed the Beavers. "Just like the Frogs. Emotional! No mind at all for practical matters!

"After all we have done for them," they would say, sitting in their comfortable lodges chatting over drinks of poplar juice, "they should be grateful."

"All the animals should be grateful," the Beavers would say. "Without us the standard of living in the Swamp would collapse."

But the other animals weren't and the Beavers decided that something should be done about it.

Many discussions were held.

It was suggested, for example, that they might invite some of the other animals in for drinks of poplar juice.

One or two might even be made members of the Beaver Club!

Finally, they came up with positively the best idea they had ever had.

"We will have a flag!" they announced, "and this will unite the Swamp."

But the Swamp had never had a flag and the Beavers were not sure what one should look like, so they had a great debate.

They talked and they talked and they talked.

They had competitions.

They argued.

And down at the Legion Lodge they even had fights.

Finally it was decided.

The Flag would be a red maple leaf on a square of thin white birch bark.

With loving care it was put together and a great holiday was declared to celebrate the first raising of the new Flag to the top of the Grand Council Lodge.

The Beavers were delighted!

The Frogs, unfortunately, had become bored with the debate and, in the meantime, had adopted the lily as their emblem. The lily, you see, was the emblem used by Frogs everywhere and they came to feel that it meant more to them than the maple leaf.

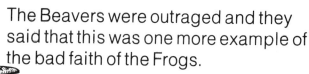

The Beavers were outraged and they said that this was one more example of the bad faith of the Frogs.

"After all, we went to this trouble mostly for them," they said.

"They should be grateful," said the Lady Beavers in their expensive fur coats.

But they weren't and one night a group of fanatic Frogs built a deadfall and the next morning a Beaver was found caught in it and badly damaged.

A wave of indignation swept the Swamp. For the first time, the Beavers began to take the Frogs seriously. Immediately, as in all crises, they appointed an Almighty Commission to investigate.

After many months, the Almighty Commission reported that the answer lay in learning the Frogs' language.

"That will make them happy," said the Almighty Commission, "and then they will be grateful."

LE...er...CROAK ?

So the Beavers, diligent in all things, tried to learn the Frogs' language.

They tried.

    And they tried.

        And they tried.

They took long hours off from their important work on the dam and cutting down trees and running the Swamp.

They were to be found everywhere, sitting round in circles, making Frog-like noises.

They tried

    And they tried.

        And they tried.

But it wouldn't work.

They couldn't talk Frog!

Worst of all, the Frogs laughed at them.

This outraged the Beavers.

"After all our efforts, they should be more appreciative," the Beavers said.

But they weren't, and the chorus at the shallow end became deafening.

Sep-ar-*ate!*

    Sep-ar-*ATE!*

        SEP-AR-*ATE!!*

But the Beavers were still only slightly worried.

"After all," they said over drinks of poplar juice, "we still control the dam."

Then it happened.

The Frogs learned how to build their own dam!

Up at the shallow end they worked on it, month after month, all by themselves, and when it was finished even the Beavers had to admit that it was a good dam. And there, behind it, was the Frogs' very own pond!

The Frogs were terribly proud—and the Beavers were consternated. The Frogs had done it!

"What shall we do?" cried the Beavers.

"Let them go!" replied some.

"Let them fuddle duddle," said others, using a phrase popular at the time.

"But if the Frogs go, then the Water Rats will go, and the Otters and the Gophers and all the others. And then the Eagles will get us all!"

And the Beavers began to wish they had been nicer to the other animals. They wished they had got to know the Otters and the Gophers better. They wished they hadn't been so mean to the Turtles.

"We will all be lost!" they cried, slapping their tails in despair.

But then, as though by magic, a wonderful Frog arrived at the Council lodge and said that he could save the Swamp. He was rich and handsome and had travelled the world, and he knew many things.

"In particular," said the Beavers, who were not without a certain cunning, "he will know how to handle the other Frogs."

So, gratefully, they made him Chief Minister of all the Swamp.

His name was Peter E. Waterhole, and he was a great success. He was strangely attractive and at once he enchanted the Lady Beavers, whose male companions were, frankly, pretty dull.

"He is our Prince Charming!" they trilled, and delicious shivers went all the way from their whiskers down to their flat tails.

Peter Waterhole went everywhere in the Swamp kissing girl Beavers and performing wonderful feats.

He was the finest swimmer and diver in all the Swamp—jackknives, swan-dives, somersaults and one-and-a-half gainers!

He sang. He danced. He carried a rose in his teeth. Even the male Beavers grudgingly admired him.

It seemed that there was nothing he could not do. He was truly the Wonder Frog!

So the Beavers once again were happy and the Chief Minister made them happier still when he married a radiant Otter princess. It was just like a fairy tale!

FRESH PICKED
LOTUS
BLOSSOMS

Now the Otters lived on the west side of the Swamp below the dam, where the water tumbled through a rocky gorge out to a lovely lake. They considered themselves the most fortunate of animals, and they thought that life behind the dam must be unbearably dull.

They played and fished and became rich, and the only thing that bothered their careless lives was the way the Beavers kept shutting their water off. This bothered them a lot.

Their neighbours, the Gophers, who lived in a sandy sort of place nearby, were even more unhappy. They were unhappy about the grasshoppers who ate the grass which they needed for food, and they were unhappy about the drought which killed the grass. These disasters, and many others, they blamed on the Beavers.

"It's all the fault of the Beavers and their dam," the Gophers said.

But the Beavers were oblivious.

For them, all life centred on the dam and they expected the other animals to be as interested in it as they were.

"The dam helps everyone and everyone should help the dam," they said cheerfully.

The other animals, however, were unconvinced and the Frogs were particularly suspicious. The Chief Minister, however, had an answer.

"What we need," he said, "is a Constitution. We shall call together the most learned animals in the Swamp and we will write new rules. Then all will be well."

In the past, the Beavers had never had much confidence in words written on pieces of birch bark, but now they became convinced that if only the *right* words could be found, the Swamp would be saved.

Many meetings were held at which animals skilled in such matters tried to find the magic combination.

They tried.

And they tried.

And they tried.

But the words which suited the Beavers did not suit the Frogs and sometimes the words proposed by the Otters did not suit either the Beavers or the Frogs.

No one listened to the Muskrats or the Water Rats or the Gophers.

And the Turtles were not even invited.

It was all very difficult and frustrating and the animals began to notice, as time went by, that Peter Waterhole was becoming less and less charming.

He no longer carried a rose in his teeth.

He no longer went around kissing girl Beavers.

And up at the shallow end, the Frogs became more and more unhappy.

Rumors flew.

It was said that a Frog Liberation Army was ready to strike.

Frogman units were said to be everywhere.

"How shall we keep the peace?" the Beavers cried.

"Call out the army!" said some.

"But armies are not good at keeping the peace," said others.

Everyone was very frightened. In this crisis, Peter Waterhole announced that he had a new plan.

"We shall have an Election," he proclaimed. "Elections are the very best thing for keeping the peace."

"We shall decide how the Swamp is to be run and who is to run it. Then all will be well."

So it was decided that the animals would choose between Peter Waterhole; Lugubrious J. Standfast, a lobster who had somehow arrived from the farthest, shallowest, easternmost end of the Swamp; and Don Quickoats, a Muskrat whose mother named him after being inspired by the noble words on the side of a cereal box so that he grew up to be a strong and vigorous champion tilting against the forces of evil.

Peter said that the animals should all vote for him because everything in the Swamp was perfect and that, in future, he would make it even better.

Lugubrious J. Standfast said they should vote for him because he was Moderate. Never having done much of anything in the past, it was unlikely he would do anything wrong in the future. Many of the animals, in particular the rich Beavers, said this was very wise. Unfortunately, Lugubrious made the mistake of addressing the Frogs in Frog, which meant that they were unable to understand him and he failed to get enough votes.

Don Quickoats said that everyone should vote for him because of his Idea which was that the dam should be owned by all the animals instead of just by the rich Beavers. But he called the rich Beavers "bums," which made them angry and led them to tell the poor Beavers not to vote for him. Since the rich Beavers were rich it was assumed that they were wise, and the poor Beavers did as they were told. So Don Quickoats was not elected.

Peter Waterhole didn't get enough votes either. In fact, when all the pieces of birch bark were counted, it was found that there was a tie between Peter and Lugubrious.

No one had won.

The Swamp was more disunited than ever!

No one knew what to do.

Even John Diefenboomer, the Great Orator, was at a loss for words.

But Peter Waterhole had a new and even better plan. There would be another election and this time, he said, the animals would recognize their folly and give him enough votes.

But this election turned out to be worse than the first one. It ended in a *three-way* tie!

In exasperation, Peter left on a long canoe trip.

Lugubrious announced that he was holding himself in readiness but no one was sure what he was ready for.

Don Quickoats didn't know what to do. He could share power with Lugubrious and the rich Beavers and thus he might be able to Do Good. Or he could stay out of power and maybe not do so good.

No one knew what to do, and things got worse and worse. The animals began to say that it was the End of the Swamp.

Then, at this black moment, a most wonderful thing happened.

The voice of a Turtle was heard in the Swamp.

It was the Chief of the Turtles, very old and very wise, who climbed to the top of the Grand Council Lodge.

"You are all mad!" he shouted.

"Do you not see that you cannot unite a swamp? Nor can you separate a swamp.

"You can only live in it. And you can love it—or you can destroy it.

"In the days of my ancestors, the Swamp was a paradise, but now the trees are cut down and the waters are dark.

"You must live once again in harmony with the Swamp. Then all will be well because those who love the Swamp also love one another.

"So, as it was long ago, let the animals look after their affairs in the places where they live.

"Let the Frogs arrange things in the shallow end.

"Let the Beavers arrange things in the deep end.

"Let the Otters and the Gophers be in charge of the places where they live because they know these places best.

"Let the Muskrats and the Water Rats have a greater voice.

"Honor your trust with the Turtles.

"And, from time to time, let us meet at the Council Lodge.

"Above all," he concluded, "remember that the Swamp has no problems—the only problem is with ourselves."

In the silence that followed, all that could be heard was the wind in the trees and the lapping of the water.

Suddenly it all seemed so simple.

So they did as the old Turtle
suggested . . .

. . . and lived surprisingly happily
ever after.

The wise old Turtle was acclaimed as a
hero and became Governor-General of
the Swamp.

Peter Waterhole became a guru in the
western wilderness where he was .
much admired for his wisdom and his
ability on the Otter slides. So he was
happy too.

There was still, however, the problem of the Paranoid Eagles. But one day the animals sensed that something was different. The Beavers paused at their work. The Frogs stopped singing and arguing. The Otters stopped playing.

And then they realized what it was—the Eagles had gone!

Not an Eagle anywhere in the poplars.

Not an Eagle in the sky.

Where had they gone?

As the animals were wondering, a squirrel came flying through the tree-tops with the news:

"The Chief Eagle has fallen!

"The Chief Eagle has fallen!

"The Chief Eagle has fallen from his tree and ruptured himself. He will never fly again. All the Eagles have gone home for the crisis!"

And they never came back.

So all was well with the Beavers and the Frogs and the Otters and all their animal friends, and they lived happily ever after.

. . . Until the day the Eagles started to
drain the Swamp.